S. D. C

Áxo

Ax

Áxonas

Axis

S. D. Curtis

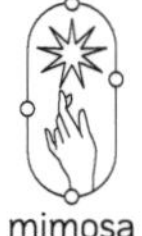

First published in 2024
by *mimosa*,
an imprint of Istros Books
London, United Kingdom
www.istrosbooks.com

Design and layout:
pikavejica.com

Illustrations:
courtesy of Alfred M. Bruckstein

Printed by CMP,
Poole, Dorset, UK

ISBN: 978-1-912545-41-4

Contents

Foreword

"How else could it have occurred to man to divide the cosmos, on the analogy of day and night, summer and winter, into a bright day-world and a dark night-world peopled with fabulous monsters, unless he had the prototype of such a division in himself, in the polarity between the conscious and the invisible and unknowable unconscious?"

(C.G. Jung, *Collected Works*)

Susan Curtis' collection of lyric poems is a stunning achievement. The clarity of her voice and the clarity of her vision spans time: from past, present and into the future, to a space where myth, metaphor and symbol are handled with such depths of feeling and intelligence to allow these poems to lead us to discovery and revelation. It is the myth-poetic voice, where myth is sacred history that returns us to ourself. It is an exploration of the reality of the imagination and the imagination of reality.

Curtis is a very perceptive image maker. The rollcall of Goddesses is numerous and fascinating, starting with the very first poem in the book, *Daphne*, where she states her aim to 'create symbol from suffering':

Hunted by the God of disease as well as healing
Daphne took refuge in the form of a tree
Brittle bark grew, like a second skin across
her mouth and breasts.
Her toes curled earthwards to dig soil,
gripping and probing into roots
...

One of the major themes in this collection is the power of the body, and the fact that the body has memory. And we see and hear in the voice of *Chiron / My Left Foot* the Centaur part man part horse, especially noted for his kindness and the wisest of beings, 'the moment of wounding'. Curtis knows that moments of trauma, moments of wounding, are moments that open to moments of healing. She knows well her Jung and the wisdom of his feeling, which now animate the gathering of her wisdom of experience.

In *Áxonas/Axis*, the engaging I-Voice in so many of these poems brings them up close to the reader. These are Tone Poems which ring with the intimacy of closeness; they so strike the eye and the ear. What they are showing us is how the light and the dark lie down together, so that there is a space set aside for our own healing and inevitably, for the forgiveness of others, for there is heart-warming tenderness here too. And these wonderful moments of astonishment to behold. Images of lyric intensity: *I hold the word 'Archaeology' under the curve of my tongue / The mind's leap and drive. / Red first meant berry, and rose, sheer rock / and beetles on sand / The curved tongue of the sea.*

Curtis understands that what cannot be imagined cannot be. She is well versed in Jungian depth psychology and technique that gives her insight into that great space behind words. She composes out of this psychoanalytic trope, knowing that the Unconscious is always making the invisible, visible. These are such poems of that making here (*Medusa, Archaeology* and *Alchemy* all appeared in the UK Jungian Journal, *Harvest*, 2022), as Curtis looks at and into the art of Alchemy symbolically, where the symbol is endlessly creative, noting that the Philosopher's Stone is how matter is turned into Spirit. This is the Journey of Soul-Making. The quest of this collection is that of Individuation: to become the person you were meant to be. And the poems ask that Archetypal question: how is it that we are so mysterious to ourselves and to the world out there?

> *"People will do anything, no matter how absurd, in order to avoid facing their own souls. One does not become enlightened by imagining figures of light, but by making the darkness conscious."*
>
> (C.G. Jung, *Psychology and Alchemy*)

Michael Harlow,
poet and Jungian therapist
Alexandra, New Zealand, 2023.

Áxonas/Axis

Daphne

Hunted by the god of disease as well as of healing,
Daphne took refuge in the form of a tree.
Brittle bark grew, like second skin across
her mouth and breasts.

Her toes curled earthwards to dig soil,
gripping and probing into roots.
The sweat of the chase condensed to sap,
as her legs twisted to trunk and her arms sought
the spheres of the sun, and the moon
within the embrace of land and heaven.

Seeking the gravity of wood, the inertia of rootedness,
she must have remembered that wind still
ruffles leaves and bends extremities.
Constant movement, even in fixedness.
And her diadem of victory was a swirl of starlings
come to sudden rest in her branches.

We have only flesh to offer –
soiled mouths, fumbling touch –
unlike gods, who kiss
the living fibre of nature,
create symbol from suffering,
metaphor from muscle.

Anagnorisis
Recognition

One moment of peace
home from school, unexpected.
My mother, kneeling by the fire
my father, letting go at the door
The retreating swirls on the carpet
pulling us towards high windows,
the light.

Something lost, then
between that quiet afternoon
and what came after it.

How once, at the beach,
I was taken by the waves,
manhandled by the current,
rolled with the sea until
up was no longer sky
nor downwards, firmness.
Breathless, I resurfaced only
to find another beach.
My family far away.

How often did I attempt
to recreate that day:
my holy trinity
of mother, father, daughter.
But the waves

had had their way.
It was a foreign shore.
And repetition alone,
could not restore
that brief harmony.
Nor could blind love,
guide me back
to light, integrity,
the fire aglow.

How could I know then
that my Ithaca
was leagues distant
and that ships
always sail straight ahead,
even when returning home.

Nostalgia

Malarial infection
of breast bone
stroking sickness
of the clavicles
ending abrupt
at the twin guards
of the throat
harbouring tearful globs
of undigested
possibilities
the sweat and release
of a glandular fluid
of intuited promises
unrealised
or spoken ones
not honoured
that dormant base note
of fever in the ditty
of normality
imperceptible
to ear and microscope
lurking in unexpected lulls
with the contracted muscle
of symphonic crescendo
a fever of memory

and regret
phantasm of home
and ache for voyages
never sailed.

Chiron

My Left Foot

Between the hilltops of rockery and the shores of the fishpond
the homeland of our small selves was as large as a savannah.
Our own private topography of hiding places,
fenced corners, bushy hollows, low sills and gradating angles.
In that endless terrain we cowboyed long afternoons
wigwamed shelters from sheets and frameless tents
while the whitewashed house stood,
a blank observer.
Its glass eyes, unseeing as I let fall the rake
between my tiny toes.
My Father blamed me for the blood that ran,
casting the genie of guilt within the tight bottle
of my immature womb.
And later, Eve-like, I bled out the sin
month by month
until that wounded foot tripped me once again
as my femininity stubbed itself
on the blunt threshold of uncut manhood
and the legacy of misplaced weight
came tumbling down the stairs.

Notes on a Hanging

I'd been hanging
out of the window
for so long. Holding fast to the sill
for all my life's worth,
my legs dangling
above the flat roof. Toes longing
for the fearful thud
of solid ground.

Did no-one think to look for me
when they found the bed empty?
I was so small
too young for flight,
for plans and destinations.
Or did they glance through the open frame,
at the long view, ignoring.
For by lowering myself down,
I had become invisible, enabled the averted gaze.

The strain of an aborted fall,
of un-executed escape,
is perhaps greater than the expected shock
of the horizontal.
But I am taller now and the ground
is nearer my feet than my head.
Yet always such small faith
in the benefits of gravity.

An aborted fall,
that strain of escape
un-executed,
is perhaps greater than
the expected shock
of the horizontal
for we grow taller
and the ground
nearer our feet
while Truth, like gravity
draws us home
to earth

Medusa
Silent Gaze

Cursed by a goddess
born from the head
of the supreme male
her secret locked behind
a frenzy of venomous mouths,
none of which hold her voice

nor recount the words
that strain from her mouth.
Only her eyes speak
of fury or fear or the fate
of those who have innocence
ripped from their bellies.

She knows the malediction well,
accepts her wordless stare
wields the petrifying power of silence,
that her eyes can never be met
nor her essence understood.
And Perseus knows too,
that truth, unacknowledged,
reflects guilt back on the victim.

But from her blood
and the sperm of sea-foam
springs Pegasus
freed of human vocabulary

through the power of instinct,
releasing muscle
into the joy of flight
and divine liberty.

Trauma

Our Deepest Wounds

In muted shades of sepia,
in fleshy folds, proceeding
hours and minutes, the rhythm
of ticks and tocks.
A *pastpresentcircle* of time
– this mortal coil –
slipping slowly, sliding southwards
along the furrows of muscle fibre,
the tautness of tendons,
into the soft balloons of organs,
the fluid universe of cells.
For water remembers
and muscles have memory.
Come – let us journey together,
down barely-lit channels
hushed with neglect
and the airlessness of avoidance.
This voyage must end,
at the beginning,
teasing out
the stain of terror.
Gently, gently,
weaving back the thread
of Selfhood
with the courage of
tenderness.

The Japanese have a knowledge
of the beauty of broken things.
A golden joinery
of edges realigned. Remembering
that distance gives geography
and altitude renders fissures
invisible.

The art of broken things
presupposes
the knowledge
that distance gives
the immaculacy of geography

the golden joinery
of edges realigned
fissures rendered invisible

Thus, the gods look down on us.

Persephone

Plucked
by unnatural desire
from the summer of youth,
the gaping space widening
beneath your solidity,
the opening of the earth
beneath your smooth feet.

Plunged
into the blackness
of all that is not known
and perhaps, unmentionable
to those who have not crossed
the frontiers of consciousness.

Imposed
on your mind
were the duality
of darkness and light
palaces of ice
and ballrooms
of golden harvest,
joint Goddess of death
and of fertility.

Algos
Pain

Pain narrows imagination
rolls it thinly into coils
of consternation
contracted by joy remembered,
hope neglected.
Losing sight of the fire,
we cannot recall heat,
nor the fresh crunch of snow,
for fear of avalanche
or traffic.
Rigor Mortis
of the blood's flow
and dance, the mind's
leap and dive.
Only the long horizon
can sometimes trigger
the thaw, allow feeling
to return to touch
and tread, freeing our
dreams from the locks
of pain, un-comprehended.
Of absence, un-bidden.

Archaeology
Somatics

As if I always knew
that beneath my skin
lay a skeleton of secrets
I held the word *archaeology*
under the curve of my tongue
like a stone dredged from a
river basin or the terminal moraine
of the ice-flow that gouged
– inch – by – inch –
through the trunk of me.

I pronounced its strangeness
with the weight of prophecy,
an alien form dropped
into a suburban garden.
With the gentlemanly pursuit
of *antiquarianism*
denied me, I dug inwards
where muscle wraps bone
– as paper, stone –
accentuating contour and curve.

Thrusting my resolute hands
deep into the earth of
flesh, where the flow
of joy had mixed with
the sediment of sorrow

to form internal strata,
the ascent and decline
of empires built between our talk,
and our dreaming sleep.

Excavation is simpler
than the task of reconstruction,
that patient re-piecing,
that detailing back the whole.
And the fossils that remain
of ancient monsters
are never the deceit of rock
but pure true memory,
waiting for hands skilled
in the art of restoration.

Soma
(After Cavafy)

Body, remember your silent rebellion
the warning nerve, like a radar
registering the shifting ground of delusion
– the voice that trembled for fear of you –
while the topological teachings
of your twistings, tested how far
pain could distort, yet still retain the shape of me.
Now remember, body, that gentler way,
a correspondence of curves and angles
diagonals of emphasis, a balancing
of bones and intention.
Together we shall chart a new course
and remember the landscape of pretence
as a shepherd remembers the storm.

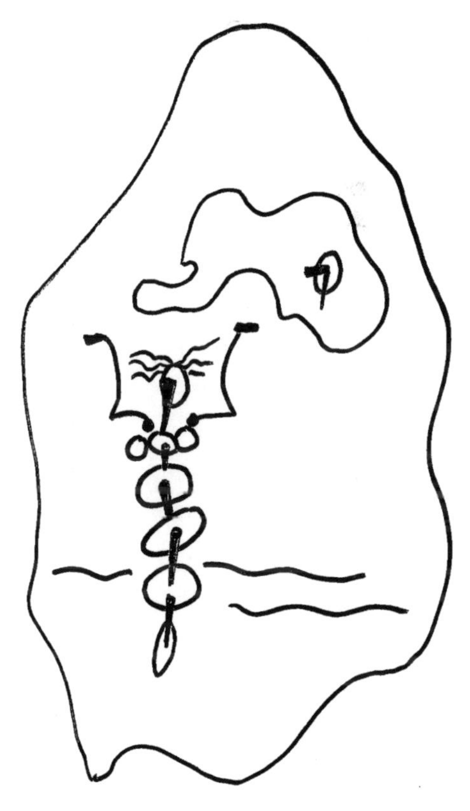

Arche

We are Water Creatures

Water is given shape
by pouring into
temperature grants it
form or flight
its bodilessness
yet has intestines
currents and movements
of its own, internal
vortexes and swirls of direction
that invigorate
in rivers, seas, oceans
the waters of the earth,
amniotic fluid
drunk in, released out,
holding form
for our own flesh,
holding memory
and remembrance
we live and sleep
tracing filaments
of light in water
living for synapses
where intention sparks
movement,
thought, genesis.

Water holds all
Air caresses it
Earth cradles.

Archai

My Four Elements

Wool for my grandma
dense caverns of intimacy
wrapped in balls of bound yarn

Asphalt for schooling
the long straight road
of leave-taking and homecoming

Hair for my own self
warm to cool through the fingers
diffuse and countless in my mouth

Salt by the falling tearful
palm-fulls on my tongue
sea-fulls on storm days

I bit down on guilt
journeying to the very roots
wool, asphalt, hair and salt

Surrendering to the sphere of story
for disparate things to combine
love and loneliness, authenticity and pain.

Wound and salve, rupture and join.

Alchemy

To form the philosopher's stone
take the breath of possibility
the fire of love, all-consuming,
the burnt earth of unhappy childhood
and the cooling water of compassion.

Once formed inside, remove
the stone from your mouth,
dissolve the solidity of silence
that weighs, like a bomb,
behind the arches of your teeth
in order to talk, and allow
the words to form in others.

This calcified mass of latent intent
dissipates like dandelion seeds
– pregnant with undercurrent –
launching from pursed lips.
But beware! This rock is as old
as a covenant, broken.
It remains unremitting
though soft as puffed promise.

Before fear breaks the spell
and forces the shards to stick
like asbestos to your limpid heart
permit that pump to beat

its true symphony
with the shadow of that mouth-stone in one hand,
and the butt of your raised sword
in the other.

Persephone II

Plucked by your uncle
after too few summers in the sun
(*Ah, so often the uncle wandering in places
he has no right to be*)
So soft the pull of earth
and the folds of your sex
Till softness collapsing
split rock, spilt soil
Exchanging darkness for light
enclosure for freedom.

But the world cannot survive
the prolonged winter
of your departure
Joint dominion was yours
palaces of ice and ballrooms
of golden harvest
Duality embedded in the godhead
of death and fertility
The burst of spring necessitating
the cold loneliness of gestation
The piqued individuality
of each blade of grass
germinating in dank earth.

And the choice is not yours
as to the place you call home

Incest is the privilege of gods,
but return, the privilege of the brave
Your uncle-husband casts shadow
to your sun, your absence
an underground presence
Autumn balanced by spring,
despair by discovery.

Wine-Dark Sea
(For Homer)

Red first meant berry,
and rose, or skin split.
Black, sheer rock and
beetles, on sand.
The white of the eyes
distinguishable against the
brown of the iris.
All that could be held,
stroked, extinguished,
could claim name to itself,
while Homer's sea and sky
remained nameless,
unknowable and therefore
unutterable beyond
the borders of self.
In the taxonomy of essentials
must thought, then word
sever the umbilical
for language to comprehend
that clouds move independently
of our wishes across
a hued infinity
and that the wet caress
of liberation from gravity
has a colour other
than our own blood?

Blue

Out of the blue
of petals. The velvet trickle
of vein. The curved tongue
of sea, jutting into
a smiling shore.
The sky that oozes
into the spaces between objects
church bells, parallel walls
– the fingers of your hand –
Blue pursues even
the smallest of animals
out of their shells and burrows.
Hounds us with billowing
infinity. And the intimate
of bruises and burning alcohol.
Accept this blue,
instead of answers,
in place of apology,
in lieu of atonement.

Entheos

The Joy Within

The God impulse
forever shunning endings
that deny the whole
the integrity of the thread
with each knot
not a failure
but a perplexity
awaiting just patience
and soft untangling
with the oiling of compassion.

Following the flow of tears
and the passage of days
without restraint or check
comes the mercy of truth
touched ever so lightly
to avoid burning
fingertips and eyelashes
on the mantle of the Divine.

Echo

Looking down on you from the rim of a well
a crescent of light from above
before the plunge to darkness towards an unknown depth.
Your face upturned, familiar
yet blurred by distance.
Only raindrops can measure that fall,
in glottal stops, our voices hardly carry,
and then there is the danger of distortion.
Yet you should know of the grass and trees
and sunshine here,
the breezes and vast horizon.
But my words cannot pass nor conjure subtle magic
from that dark place.
The stagnation of depths not plummeted,
long un-comprehended, throws back echoes.
Words aimed at others, return home to the self
and eyes go blind, so long unseeing.

Words aimed at others
always
return to haunt us
setting free ghosts
that blur our vision.

Hermetic Arts
Divination

I climbed the rungs
– each by turn –
of that promised destiny
Stopping at every stage
to check the view
and search the horizon
for your form.

I prayed for love and healing
and received only silence.
My proud, yearning heart
wound itself out and in again.
Now soft, now sinuous,
aging with each undulation.

Stranded like a jellyfish
beneath each heave
and pull of the water
inside me. The tides
that measure my worth
by love spent
and returned.

It seems I've climbed
for years and lifetimes
my sight and hearing
in your service.

Will I look for you still
knowing that my forgiveness
may not preclude
your penance?

Narcissus

When you look
into the green irises
of my blue eyes
you see the smooth
reflective surface
of trauma, inverted
of love, perverted.
At the shore
of this wide body of water
reflected sky belies
depth, reflected gaze
belies possession.

And that which glitters,
on the crystalline surface,
belies the creases and crevices
of all our avoidances,
the ravages of repression
borne too long.
Are we destined, then,
to suicide of the self
or can the image of
that flower,
with its golden cup,
contain new existence?
The peace of immobility

52 The end of fleeing,
and the wordlessness
of completion.

Would that I Could

Would that I could
return to those days.
The girl in her room
drawing with crayons
her masterpieces
of unselfconsciousness.
The man at work
winning the bread.
My story still nestled
inside my breast
like a cyst the weight
of an acorn.
Could I have left
the field fallow
or had the sap of life
already stirred its sides
unstoppable as raucous spring
after the frosted peace
of prolonged winter.
The girl no longer draws
her room is empty
the loaves gone stale
for want of moisture
or the gaze of desire.
And yet the scene plays on
under the branches
of my narrative
grown tall and wild.

A Silent Death

Without the luxury of twin mouth
to bargain with
nor face to witness except the mirrored self,
there is no place to go
but the inside of things
soft underbelly of childhood
pincushions of playgrounds
glimpses in transit
of words half understood.
We can wait for so long
into the future
for that which may never arrive
from the past.
We can long for changes
that may come only
when we have turned our backs.

Prometheus

The gift of fire
gives light, heat
and night vision.
Grants us flames
that render substance
to ashes, intentions
to regrets, or illuminate
the dark cave that stretches
behind us, where the bones
of fallen prey stretch across
textured recesses,
and the sharp crags
of overhangs lie,
unforeseen.

Bound to the rock of truth
deprived of shelter
from the eagle's beak
or the vengeance of those
who shun the warmth
for fear of the furnace,
Prometheus waits
for the courage of Hercules,
to set him free.

Aphiēmi
Unburdening

I’ve left my burden
– my cartload, my haul –
in the middle of the road
to sit alone on the bank.

The traffic, I know
is inconvenienced
but my skin is warm
comforted by its own edges

honouring the feelings
– private, childlike, stubborn –
that have taken my hand
and demand audience

this small dialogue
may last just a second
or as long as a seed
takes to grow roots.

Have patience here
do not raise the limb
of exasperation, or voice
to the demands of transport

Greet me as your kin
new and already known
when this conversation
invites the other back in.

Silence Shapes Us

Here is the silence
you've avoided so long.

Here is the rock
you didn't dare to tread.

Here is the sea
whose depth hides in shadow.

Gather your skirts
remove your shoes
and grip your toes.
Befriend loneliness
to call it solitude.

No man becomes himself
without a time of internment.
No woman becomes great
without freeing herself
from making meaning for man.

Silence billows around doors
creeps under windows
in fearful wisps of nostalgia.
Stand your ground.
Remember that sea wears rock
and rock forms the waters.

Agapē
No Earthly Love

Once I sought
across the purple skies
in the wake of planes
and the trajectory of birds
for traces of your love,
for the reassurance of meaning,
just as once we looked
for augury
in the bowels of owls,
the steaming remains
of creatures cut down,
still hot from the effort
of escape, whereas
your entrails are cold
and the rusted trail of blood
points only to eternity,
the Calvary of acceptance
the shroud stained
with faith, and the power
of sacrifice demanded
and paid.

Aphiēmi
Untethering

The Gordian knot
of tangled intention
and frayed promises
slashed in one blow by
precise incision, bladed resolve.
The moment grasped,
meaning pinned with clarity
of foresight, balanced
perfectly with hindsight
that sweet axis beyond
the logic of sums and science
in spite – or in sight –
of prophecy
so quickly sharp there is
no pain, just the single
stroke of decision
and the slow
slow,
slide of blood.

Archaeology II
Digging

As I weed out the seeded plants
from those that will survive
I find smooth stones
and grooved shells
that your hands planted
along with roots and bulbs.
Soft chalky contours
reveal themselves in dark earth
their legless surrender
to the surface, touching
a ripple across the skin,
soft vibration of nostril
against the odour of sweat
barely remembered.
Calcified antler
and jaw bone
of another species
outrun, out-hunted
through heedless seasons.
Between barrow and trowel
my hand lingers
grants grace to mechanisms
that grasped, thrust,
smoothed over. Amnesty,
to what has been extinguished
and that which remains.

Moirologia
Lamentation

Mourning is the prerogative
we grant to the dead
and of all that has passed away
Antigone knew too well
that the rights of the deceased
outweighed those of the living,
and that unsung things brought
the wrath of furies
and gods avenging.
Elektra damned the mother
who buried a king,
un-mourned.

So women carry the burden
of sorrow. Verse themselves in the only
poetry permitted to their tongues.
Acknowledged by the Greeks
as carriers of the male seed
and channels through which
things flow, from nature to men
and even, perhaps, to heaven.
The hollowness of their throats,
the transparency of their skin,
the trill of their cries, alone,
accompanied the corpse
across the river Styx.

Their voices then, give shape
to grief, their bodies bear
the duty of atonement.
Their hands sow and knead
and stuff the meaning
into bread and effigies,
from the morning of birth
to the evening of death,
along with their singing
of the achievements of men
that would be gods
and kings.

Our Mothers

We wear our mothers' regrets
like raincoats saved for autumn storms.
Their flimsy material worn thin,
they serve us poorly as we
wriggle to fit our own limbs into
the measurements of another's
habits and reaches.

The movements we have tried
so hard to avoid, appear suddenly
in our repertoire, as if hidden
in muscle and bone. The steps
of dances long out-fashioned,
dulled by music nobody remembers
in the shells of their tiny ears.

Our mothers have cast off
their smooth skins, surrendered
their menfolk along with their bleeding.
Outside the theatre of femininity,
they have no need for the
architecture of amour.
Nor the thud, thud, thud
of history repeating.

Only we still move to the rhythm
of the moon and madness,
hoping this dance is all our own.
For silence is yet too expensive,
and the noise of our mother's mistakes
are as distracting as the clamour
of our own youth, not yet laid to rest.

Heritage

The anger of my grandmother
was not the anger of my mother
but made of richer stuff.
Of the cat's search for open doors,
of the weeping women of Guernica
burning with the heat of desperation
that rises above the cool air
of indifference.
For every shirking of duty
the good take on extra load.
In the isolated territory
of the strong woman,
the Incandescence of Indignation
so coolly confused with insanity
sent our foremothers
to graves and asylums.
Their ghosts like sirens now,
urge us out to sea,
and the white-hot beauty,
of our anger.

Aphiēmi

Forgiveness

There is a space set aside
for the forgiving of our parents.
One wall is lined with mirrors,
while the floor can be grass,
earth, or the hard stuff of rock.

Long winters of hurricane
or drought will leave no mark.
For the expanse remains
intact, whether it is used or
neglected, since the beginning cannot

anticipate the end, and hope knows
to wait for the final breath before
withdrawing. The gods demand
we lay down our shields and swords,
strip from the ragged uniforms.

We alone can enter, but only they
can bestow the blessing,
revealing the alchemy of reflection
that opens other spaces within
generations past, and those to come.

Catharsis
Nocturnal Epiphanies

Woken by inner lightning
flashes of comprehension
sweet lappings
against the shores
of the subjective.
Farewells to all
that has passed,
fallen away from
the musculature of now.

(Pity the man
whose sinuous act
fails to move an audience
to comprehension
Pity the woman
whose fluid flows
only to stain
clothes and groins)

Pelvic bowl
and jaw bone
conversing
with lymphatic fluency
through tremulous
understandings
of time and space
and blood, blood, blood

all that ever bled out
and that which is left un-bled
collecting and coagulating
into new form
Child of Self.

Cassandra
Not Disbelieved, but Unheeded

When it all falls away,
the armature of stubborn No,
and the sweet angles of repose
return to your limbs
the milk and honey of release.

When the outcome
of ancient divination
tumbles down on us
with the inevitability of truth,
of liquid turned to solid.

It may well be, so very well be,
too late for us in this life.
Yet the story goes on,
passed through word of mouth,
crook of arm, tilt of head.

Passed in pauses between words
and shafts of lies and dust
that cling to words
and plant them – firm –
into memory and cell.

Each atom of revelation,
spinning electrons of epiphany,
enter our veins and arteries
on their way to the heart.
The end is where we pause
to survey the damage.

And begin again.

Corfu, with Tenderness

An old man leans on his
makeshift staff of bamboo
and stares into the distance
as still as a tree or shrub.

I see the balding peak
of his head, and his knees
slightly bent to take the strain
off his lower back.

I see him, but he is unaware
of me, as I look down from above.
Wide blue skies encompass the distance
where mountains crouch.

And further east those
snow-topped peaks of Albania
margin the spiky line
of distant cypress trees.

A clutter of cats curls and
undulates in playful romp
only when he appears in this
garden away from home.

Near enough for him to feel
their presence, yet out of arm's
reach. There will be food later
that is their secret accord.

Beyond, a circle of birds exchange
light for shade, triangles that flit
from white to dark as the flock
find their next landing.

The cocks crow, though dawn
has long passed. The last corner of sunshine
warms the balcony and I remember,
without nostalgia.

Corfu, Remembered

I recognized your geography
from the air: an inverted
bass clef, to the overture
of sea and mountain.

Walking your cobbled streets
shuttered, strung with washing
familiar notes, from Venice to Kythira.
The leitmotif of the Adriatic,
descending scales of sails and destinies:
Kapodistrias, Casanova, pietra.

Four million cypresses, they say,
five million olives, grown gnarled
and tall. Giant groves clustered
above cliff tops. The plunge to blue.

And on that first day back
a sudden revelation, a stanza
so apt, so poetic
lost in the turn of a wave. Forgotten
before it was fully formed.

Forgotten, as we forgive your sleepy chaos,
the traffic and the pot-holes,
the detritus of discarded products.
In the hope that the ocean is deep enough,
the land proficient,
our wisdom, yet still intact.